What is Easter?

Written by Phil Vischer.
Illustrated by Heath McPherson.

A *Buck Denver and Friends* Book

ISBN-13: 978-0-9886144-7-5

Printed in the United States of America.

www.whatsinthebible.com • www.jellytelly.com

WHAT IS EASTER?

Written by Phil Vischer

Illustrated by Heath McPherson

Marcy has a question. "What is Easter?"

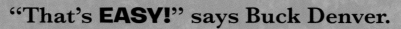

"That's **EASY!**" says Buck Denver.

"Easter is eggs!
Easter is bunnies!"

"You're forgetting something, Buck,"
says Sunday School Lady.

"Easter is all about Jesus!"

Marcy is confused. "What do eggs and bunnies have to do with **JESUS?**"

"Good question! Let's talk about winter!" says Sunday School Lady.

Now Buck is confused, too. "Winter??"

"Winter is cold.
Trees don't have leaves in winter.
Birds don't lay eggs in winter.

Rabbits don't have baby rabbits in winter.
There is no new life in winter."

"Then comes spring!
Trees have leaves!
Birds lay eggs!

Rabbits have baby bunnies!
LOTS of baby bunnies!"

"Spring is new life. And **JESUS** is new life!"

Buck and Marcy are **STILL** confused.
"How is Jesus new life?"

"Jesus said he was bringing new life.
But then he died. He was buried in a tomb.

There was no new life.
It was like winter."

"That's right!
Easter is a celebration of new life in Jesus!
His new life when he rose again,
and the new life he promises all of us!"

"I get it!" says Buck.
"Eggs and bunnies remind us of new life!"

"Right!" Marcy jumps in happily. "And Jesus brings new life! Just like spring brings new life!"

So Easter is eggs.

And Easter is bunnies.

Because eggs and bunnies remind us of new life in Jesus!

New life for ALL of us!

"I came that they may have life and have it abundantly."
John 10:10b